PRACTICE BOOK

Full Sails

Harcourt Brace & Company

Orlando Atlanta Austin Boston San Francisco Chicago Dallas New York Toronto London

SIGNATURES

CONTENTS

FULL SAILS

Printed in the United States of America

ISBN 0-15-307411-6

3 4 5 6 7 8 9 10   030   99 98 97

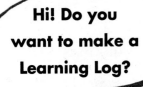

1. Get some colored paper and some white paper.

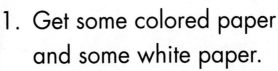

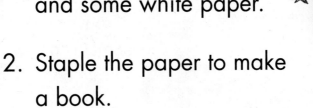

2. Staple the paper to make a book.

3. Write *My Learning Log*. Then write your name and draw some pictures on the cover.

Harcourt Brace School Publishers

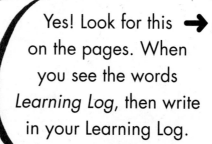

Name _____

Write the word that best completes each sentence. Then help Duck and Hen solve their problem.

The Missing Seeds

_____

- -

1. "Let's _____ a garden," said Duck.

       some   plant   into

_____

- -

2. "I will _____," said Hen.

     found   help   who

_____

- -

3. "Give me _____ seeds."

     some   asked   who

_____

- -

4. "I _____ the seeds," said Duck.

     some   into   found

_____

- -

5. "Look _____ the bag!" said Hen.

     asked   found   into

GO ON

Harcourt Brace School Publishers

"_____

6. _____ are not seeds."

Found   Help   These

_____

7. "It's _____!" said Hen.

some   flour   asked

"_____   _____

8. _____ put it here?" _____ Duck.

Help   Who   Into   asked   some   found

Who do you think put flour in the seed bag?

_____

_____

_____

_____

Name _____

Think about "The Little Red Hen." Then complete the flowchart.

The Little Red Hen

1.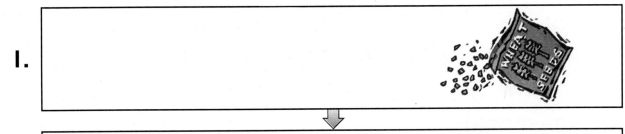

2.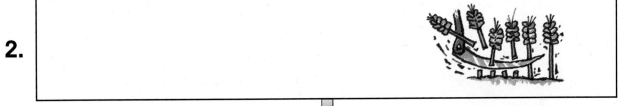

3. thresh wheat

4.

5. make flour into bread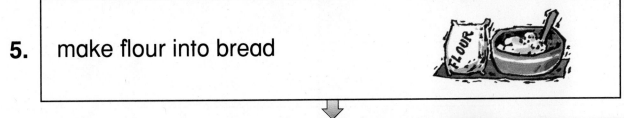

6.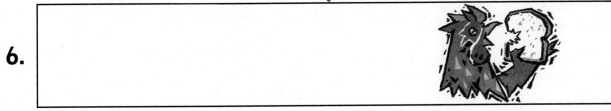

Name _____

Some naming words name the **months** of the year. The names of the months begin with capital letters. Some naming words name **holidays.** These words begin with capital letters, too.

Circle the names of the months and the holidays. Write them correctly. Then write your favorite month and holiday.

The Best Days of All
by Katie

The best day in february is valentine's day. I like independence day in july. In november thanksgiving day comes. What days do you like the best?

Months	Holidays

Name _____

A. Write the Spelling Words in their shapes. Color the boxes that have the letter *e*.

1.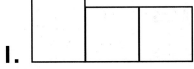

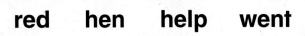

| red | hen | help | went |

2.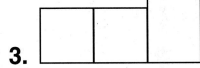

3.

4.

B. Write two Spelling Words to complete the rhyme.

_____

_ _ _ _ _ _ _ _ _ _ _ _ _ _ _ _ _ _

A boy named *Ben* has a _____.

_____

_ _

Look where it _____! It's in the *tent*.

SCIENCE

Name _____

Write the word that best completes each sentence.

flap

fly

black

Cluck

plants

_____

- -

I. Hens can be red, white, or _____.

"_____"

- -

2. They say, _____.

_____

- -

3. A hen can _____ its wings.

_____

- -

4. Hens can't _____ very high.

TRY THIS!
Learning Log

What is the same about all the words you wrote? Make a list of other words that are like these words.

Harcourt Brace School Publishers

Name _____

Look at each set of pictures. Draw what will happen next.

SCIENCE

TRY THIS!
Writing

Pick one set of pictures. Write sentences to tell a story.

**Read the words in the box. Make a check by
each thing you can find in the picture. Then draw the
things you can't find.**

web	cat	can	nest
egg	hat	grass	hen

Cut out the words. Add some words of yo
own. Make your own sentences. Then paste some o
your sentences onto a sheet of paper.

The surprise ! At last

? I woke up while . .

I must find The story ?

I found . ! Still playing

Where is ? They were

In the sky An oak tree .

VOCABULARY   **11**

at last | ! | the surprise

. | . | I woke up while | ?

? | the story | I must find

still playing | ! | . | I found

they were | ? | where is

. | an oak tree | in the sky

Harcourt Brace School Publishers

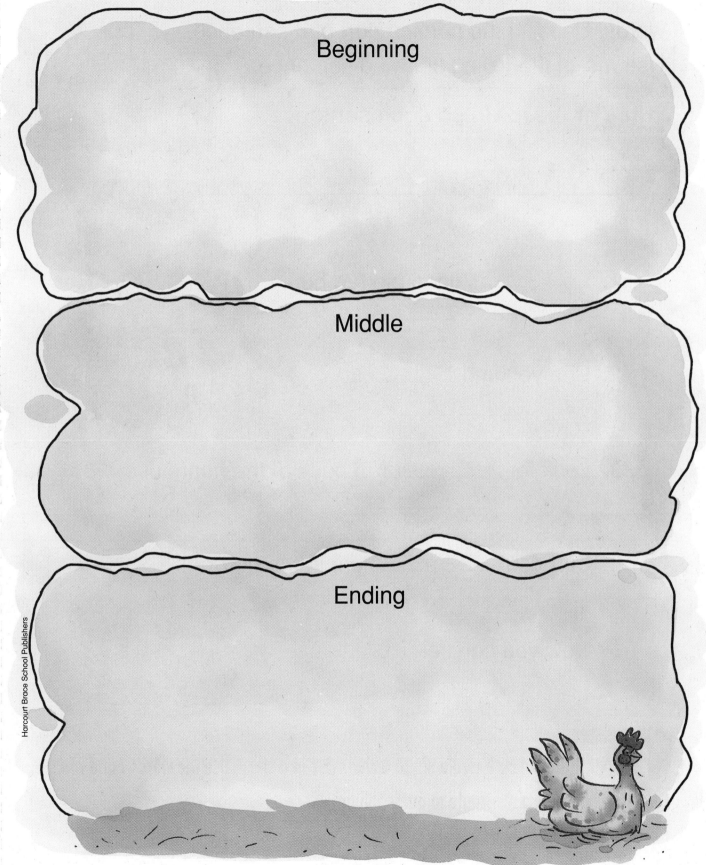

Name _____

Fill in the story frame.

Beginning

Middle

Ending

The words **I** and **me** take the place of naming words. Use **I** in the naming part of a sentence. Use **me** in the telling part of a sentence.

Write I or me to finish each sentence.

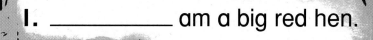

1. _____ am a big red hen.

2. Can you find _____?

3. Look for _____ in back of the henhouse.

4. Surprise! _____ am in the garden!

5. Now you can see _____!

Make up a riddle about a character in a story. Use the words *I* and *me*. Ask a classmate to guess the answer.

Name _____

A. Read the Spelling Words and say the picture names. Write the word that rhymes with each picture. Circle the letter *u* in each word.

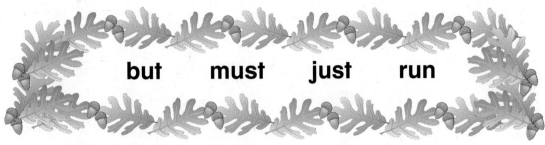

but   must   just   run

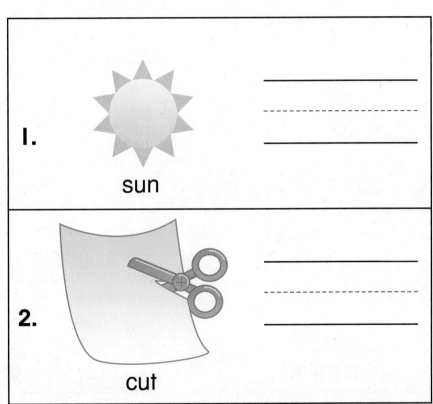

I. sun

_____
- - - - - - - - - - - - -
_____

2. cut

_____
- - - - - - - - - - - - -
_____

B. Two Spelling Words rhyme. Write these words in the correct shapes. Color the boxes that have the letter *u.*

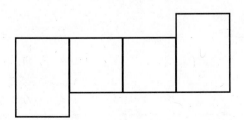

Read Henny Penny's list of things to do. Draw a circle around all the words that end with the same sound as _vest._ Then write the circled words on the chart where they belong.

Things to Do

1. Dust my nest.

2. Make a list of my best friends.

3. Rest by the oak.

4. Look at the sky. Is it falling?

5. If it is, run away fast!

These words rhyme.	These words do not rhyme.

Name _____

Write the word that best completes each sentence and has the same vowel sound as *boat*.

| stop | soap | go | dog | rope | goat |

1. One, two, three, _____!

2. Ride that _____!

3. The _____ broke.

4. Oh, no! Get some _____!

Read the names for each row of nests. Write them on the nests in ABC order. The first row is done for you.

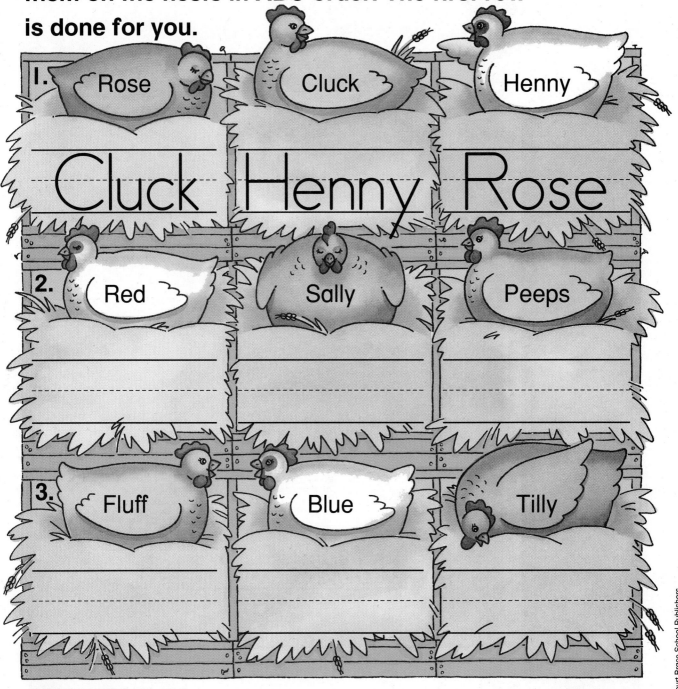

1. Rose   Cluck   Henny

   Cluck   Henny   Rose

2. Red   Sally   Peeps

3. Fluff   Blue   Tilly

TRY THIS! Writing

Write the first names of five friends. Then write the names in ABC order.

Name _____

Cut out the bricks. Then match the words to the sentences to build the word wall.

1. The _____ house is on a hill.

2. He is the king of the _____ .

3. One day the king and his friends _____ up there.

4. I could _____ if I climb up that hill.

5. I _____ would like to go see him.

GO ON

danced	king's		
still	fall		
town			

1. It is _____ my birthday.

2. My birthday party will be at _____.

3. Should I have it inside or _____?

4. I hope _____ one of my friends is there.

5. We will all have fun _____.

home	every
outside	almost
	together

Name _____

Fill in the story map.

What is Lumpty's first problem?

How does he solve it?

What is Lumpty's second problem?

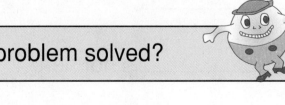

How is the problem solved?

SUMMARIZE AND RETELL **21**

The words **he, she,** and **it** take the place of some naming words. Use *he* for a man or a boy. Use *she* for a woman or a girl. Use *it* for an animal or a thing.

Read the sentences. Some words have lines under them. Write *He, She,* or *It* to stand for these words.

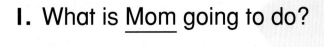

1. What is <u>Mom</u> going to do?

   _____

   _____ is going to tell a story.

2. <u>The story</u> is about an egg.

   _____

   _____ is a story I always like.

3. Now Mom is saying, "Where is <u>Ed</u>?

   _____

   _____ is not here."

4. <u>My mother</u> is looking for me!

   _____

   _____ does not know I am looking for her!

Name _____

A. Read the Spelling Words. Say the picture names. Write the word that rhymes with each picture. Circle the letter *i* in each word.

in   it   big   him

1. wig   _____

2. pin   _____

3. hit   _____

4. swim   _____

B. Write a rhyming Spelling Word in the puzzle to tell about the picture.

p
i
g

Name _____

Read each sentence. Make the word that completes the sentence, and write it on the line.

_____

1. I went _____ on a horse.

   ride + ing

_____

2. I _____ all over the place.

   dance + ed

_____

3. I _____ playing tag.

   like + ed

_____

4. I ran while my friend was _____ me.

   chase + ing

_____

5. Next we will be _____ a rest.

   take + ing

Harcourt Brace School Publishers

Little Lumpty

Name _____

Write the word that best completes each sentence and matches the picture.

hen's	dog's
bug's	pig's

This is my bed!

_____

1. A hen is on the _____ head.

_____

2. The pig is sitting by the _____ eggs.

_____

3. Is the pig on the _____ bed?

_____

4. No. The pig is on the _____ bed.

Harcourt Brace School Publishers

FULL SAILS Practice Book

POSSESSIVES: 's   **25**

Name _____

Name _____

Write words from the box to complete the riddle. Use words that have the same vowel sound as *boat*.

hole	top	home	boat	go	stop	road

_____

1. You can stop or _____ on me.

_____

2. I can take you away or take you _____.

_____

3. I may have a bump, or I may have a _____.

_____

4. A truck can ride on me, but not a _____.

_____

5. I am a _____.

Draw a map. Show the way you get to school. Draw a line on the roads from your house to the school.

Harcourt Brace School Publishers

SCIENCE

Look at the first two pictures. Circle the picture that shows what will happen next. Write a sentence about it.

I.

2.

Harcourt Brace School Publishers

Cut out the clues and word cards, and paste the pairs together. Then you and a partner can use your cards together to play "Concentration."

We are good to eat for lunch.	The little word *out* is in me.	I have two *e*'s side by side.
You can find *be* in me!	A color word is in me.	I tell how some animals are.
I'm not bad.	I look like the word *night.*	I begin like *cat.*

care	whispered	keep
wild	sandwiches	good
shouted	might	because

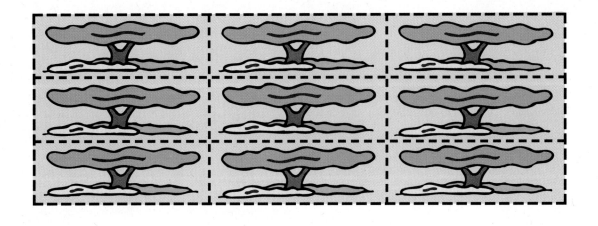

Name _____

Fill in the story frame to retell the story.

Title:	Setting:	Characters:

Beginning:

Middle:

Ending:

Harcourt Brace School Publishers

Name _____

Describing words tell about naming words.

Write a describing word for each sentence.

_____
- - - - - - - - - - - - - - - - - - - -
1. We are _____ ducks.

_____
- - - - - - - - - - - - - - - - - - - -
2. Do you like our _____ heads?

_____
- - - - - - - - - - - - - - - - - - - -
3. Look at our _____ feet!

_____
- - - - - - - - - - - - - - - - - - - -
4. We swim in _____ water.

Draw a picture of a wild animal. Tell a partner about the animal.
Use a describing word in your sentence. Then write the sentence.

Harcourt Brace School Publishers

Name _____

Read each sentence. Write the spelling word that completes each one.

when   what   where   why

1. Look at a map to find out ⬚⬚⬚⬚.

2. Look at a clock to find out ⬚⬚⬚⬚.

3. Look at a newspaper to find out ⬚⬚⬚⬚

and ⬚⬚⬚.

Write the word that best completes each sentence.

fish

what

where

show

_____
- -
1. I want to _____ you something.

_____
- -
2. This is _____ we go fishing.

_____
- -
3. Dad is catching a _____.

_____
- -
4. Look _____ I found!

Harcourt Brace School Publishers

Name _____

Write the word that best completes the sentence and has the same vowel sound as *night.*

_____

- -

1. I am a _____ animal.

        big   wild   like

_____

- -

2. Look up at the sky at _____.

        bike   day   night

_____

- -

3. You _____ see me there.

     might   ride   could

_____

- -

4. I hope I won't give you a _____.

        kiss   fright   climb

TRY THIS! Learning Log

Look at the words you wrote. How are they alike? How are they different? Write a rhyming word for each one.

Read the story. Then fill in the story map.

Mott's Birthday

Mott the Mouse was sad. Today was his birthday. He could not find any of his friends. He went for a walk in the garden. He looked at the plants. They were moving!

"Who is back there?" called Mott.

"Surprise!" shouted all his friends.

"Happy Birthday, Mott!"

"Thank you!" Mott smiled.

Who?	
Where?	
What happened first?	
What happened next?	
What happened at the end?	

Harcourt Brace School Publishers

Name _____

Draw and write what will happen next.

SCIENCE

I. Look at the eggs in the nest.
There are some cracks on them.
What will come out?

2. What is the mother bird doing?
What does she want to get?

3. What will she do now?
What will the little birds do?

Jess saw many things in the woods each day.

Help her put the things she saw in ABC order.

What Jess Saw in the Woods

Sunday	Monday	Tuesday	Wednesday	Thursday	Friday	Saturday
___ oak	___ moth	___ duck	___ mouse	___ moss	___ nest	___ ant
___ animals	___ fly	___ frog	___ nuts	___ web	___ egg	___ dog
___ plants	___ bee	___ lake	___ bugs	___ fish	___ log	___ bat

TRY THIS! Word Play

Choose three animals that can fly. Be sure each name begins with a different letter. Write them on small slips of paper. Put them in ABC order.

Name _____

Write the word that best completes each sentence.

leaves	way	feel
trees	along	

_____

1. Let's walk _____ the road.

_____

2. We can go this _____.

_____

3. Look at the branches on the _____.

_____

4. The green _____ are on the branches.

_____

5. I _____ happy out here!

Harcourt Brace School Publishers

Name _____

soft	turn	their
short	live	

_____
----

6. You can _____ left here.

_____
----

7. We have a _____ way to go.

_____
----

8. Look at the _____ little ducks.

_____
----

9. I like _____ little feet.

_____
----

10. They _____ here by the water!

Name _____

Fill in the K-W-L chart.

K	What I **K**now

W	What I **W**ant to Know

L	What I **L**earned

Name _____

Some describing words tell how people **feel.**

Write a word from the box that tells how you feel. Draw your face to match each sentence.

	sad		**happy**
	surprised		**tired**

_____

- -

1. Now I feel _____.

_____

- - - - - - - - - - - - - - - -

2. I feel _____ after I
run a very long way.

_____

- -

3. When I get a gift, I feel _____.

_____

- - - - - - - - - - - - - -

4. I feel _____ when
all the fun is over.

Harcourt Brace School Publishers

Name _____

A. Read the Spelling Words and say the picture names. Write the word that rhymes with each picture. Circle the letter *a* in each word.

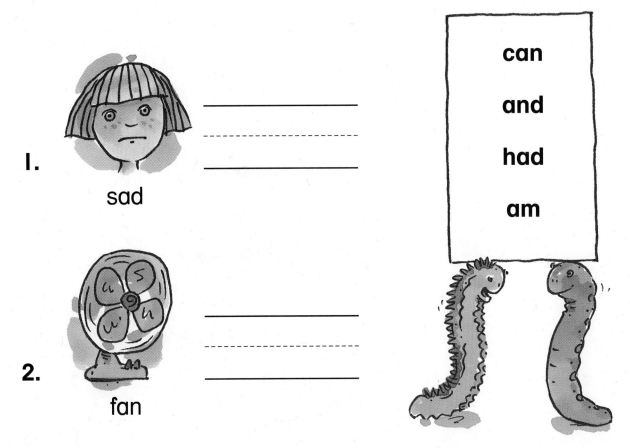

1. sad

   _____

2. fan

can

and

had

am

B. Circle the Spelling Word hidden in each word. Then write the words in their shapes. Color the boxes that have the letter *a.*

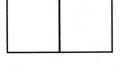

1. ham

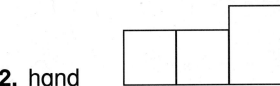

2. hand

**Write words from the box to complete the
riddle. Use words that have the same vowel
sound as *leaf*.**

| see |
| feet |
| met |
| feed |
| eat |
| queen |
| nest |

_____

- -

1. You can't _____ me.

_____

- -

2. My home is down at your _____.

_____

- -

3. I do not _____ on my own.

_____

- - - - - - - - - - - - - - - - - - - -

4. My little friends _____ me.

_____

- - - - - - - - - - - - - - - - - - - -

5. I am an ant _____.

Name _____

Read the story. Then answer the questions.

Big Worms

Most worms are about as long as your hand. But one kind can grow much longer. It lives in Australia, and it can grow to be 10 feet long. That is as long as a pickup truck.

1. What is this story about?

_____

- -

_____

2. How big do these worms get?

_____

- -

_____

3. Where do these worms live?

_____

- -

_____

Write a number sentence to show how long three Australian worms would be. Then write sentences for four worms and for five worms.

MAIN IDEA AND DETAILS 45

**Read the words and look at the boxes. Write
each word in the box where it belongs.**

wash	where	when	ship
which	what	shouted	whispered

Question Words

_____   _____
- - - - - - - - - - - - - -   - - - - - - - - - - - - - -
_____   _____
- - - - - - - - - - - - - -   - - - - - - - - - - - - - -
_____   _____

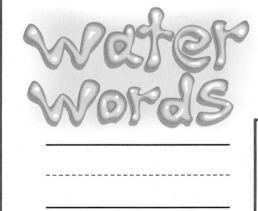

Water Words

_____
- - - - - - - - - - - - - -
_____
- - - - - - - - - - - - - -
_____

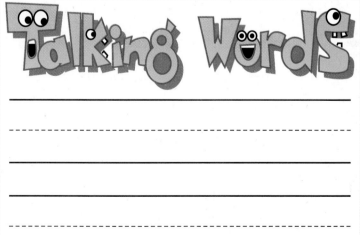

Talking Words

_____
- - - - - - - - - - - - - -
_____
- - - - - - - - - - - - - -
_____

Name _____

It's time for the Worm Games! Write all the worms' names in ABC order. Then write the names of the games in ABC order.

Worms
Mud   Buck   Rocky
Slim   Fred

1. _____

2. _____

3. _____

4. _____

5. _____

Games
Burrow   Eat   Wiggle
Dig   Hide

1. _____

2. _____

3. _____

4. _____

5. _____

Name _____

Write the word that best completes each sentence.

world   felt

wish

afraid   night

_____

1. It is day on one side of the _____.

_____

2. It is _____ here.

_____

3. Have you _____ happy at night before?

_____

4. I have! I'm not _____ at night.

_____

5. I _____ you could come out.

Name _____

ground   close

work   most

_____
- -

6. We could sit on the _____ together.

_____
- -

7. You could sit _____ to the water.

_____
- -

8. We would not do any _____.

_____
- -

9. You and I would have the _____ fun of all!

Harcourt Brace School Publishers

Name _____

Think about the story.
Then complete the chart.

What does Toad want?

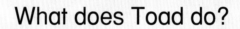

What does Toad do?

What happens in the end?

Harcourt Brace School Publishers

Name _____

Some describing words tell about **size** or **shape**.
Some describing words tell about **taste** or **smell**.

Write words from the box to complete the ad.
Draw a picture to go with the ad.

Size Words		Shape Words		Taste and Smell Words	
	little		square		sweet		smoky
	big		round		sour		fresh

EAT SOME GARDEN BITS!

_____
- -

They taste very _____.

_____
- -

They have a shape like a _____.

_____
- -

You will like their _____ smell.

_____
- -

They come in a very _____ box.

You will like Garden Bits a lot!

A. Write two Spelling Words to complete the rhyme. Circle the letter *o* in the words that you write.

on   not   stop   got

We are on *top*. Now let's _____.

Are you very *hot*? I am _____.

B. Write the Spelling Words to complete the sentence. Color the boxes that have the letter *o*.

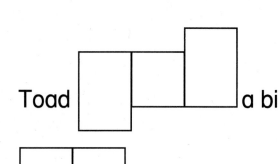

Toad ☐☐☐ a big surprise

☐☐ his birthday!

Name _____

Write the words from the box to complete the poem.

end	camp
told	champ
friend	cold

When school got out

_____

- - - - - - - - - - - - - - - - - - - -

I went to _____,
And there I met

_____

- -

The jump rope _____.

No one liked her,

_____

- - - - - - - - - - - - - - - - - - - -

I was _____,
Because she was

_____

- - - - - - - - - - - - - - - - - - -

So green and _____.

We jumped all day

_____

- - - - - - - - - - - - - - - - - - - -

And in the _____
We both had found

_____

- -

A new best _____.

FINAL CLUSTERS: mp, nd, ld **53**

SCIENCE

Name _____

Read the paragraph. Then write the word or words that best complete each sentence.

Toad Toads look like frogs, but toads live on land. They like water, too. Many toads have a gray or brown color. Toads eat many insect pests. They can be found in gardens and woods.

_____
- -

1. A toad is an _____ that lives on land.

   animal   pony

_____
- - - - - - - - - - - - - - - - -

2. Many toads have a brown or gray _____.

   color   below

_____
- -

3. A toad eats _____.

   beside   insects

_____
- -

4. You might find a toad in a _____.

   today   garden

MEDIAL CONSONANTS: /n/n, /s/s, /d/d, /l/l

FULL SAILS Practice Book

Harcourt Brace School Publishers

Name _____

Read the clues. Write the word from the box that fits the clue.

quilt	belt	plant	tent	dust
	cent	nest		

_____

- -

I. You can find me on a bed. I am a _____.

2. You can find me in a tree. I am a place for eggs.

_____

- - - - - - - - - - - - - - - - - - - -

I am a _____.

_____

- - - - - - - - - - - - - - - - - - - -

3. You might spend me. I am one _____.

_____

- - - - - - - - - - - - - - - - -

4. You can go inside me. I am a _____.

5. You can find me in the garden. I need sun and water.

_____

- -

I am a _____.

TRY THIS!
Writing

Which two words did not fit the clues? Write "You can find me" clues for those two words.

Name _____

SCIENCE

Read each sentence. Write the word that makes sense in the sentence and has the same vowel sound as _kite_.

_____

1. This frog is _____ green.

    like   bright   grow

_____

2. It sits in the pond most of the _____.

    time   day   tight

_____

3. It _____ to eat bugs.

    wants   likes   bike

_____

4. It naps in the _____.

    sunshine   water   line

_____

5. Then it croaks all _____.

    day   night   while

Read the sentences and look at the pictures. Write the word from the box that best completes each sentence.

fish	what	ship	shall
dish	shine	when	

_____
- - - - - - - - - - - - - - - - -

1. What will they want _____ they make a wish?

_____
- - - - - - - - - - - - - - - - -

2. I'll wish for a _____ of food.

_____
- - - - - - - - - - - - - - - - -

3. I'll wish for a _____.

_____
- - - - - - - - - - - - - - - - -

4. I'll wish for a _____.

_____
- - - - - - - - - - - - - - - - -

5. I know _____ I'll wish for— three more wishes!

**Write the word that best completes each
sentence to finish the rhyme.**

snow

facing   right

wasn't   _____

It _____ quite night.

scarf

The time was just _____.

I was _____ my window.
Oh, what a sight!

I put on my coat, my _____,
and my hat.

I ran out in the _____
just like that!

Harcourt Brace School Publishers

Name _____

You're

end

small

later

_____

I rode my _____ sled
around the bend.

It was lots of fun,

_____

but it had to _____.

_____

A little bit _____,
my dad came outside.

"_____

He said, _____ having fun,
but just one more ride."

Name _____

Fill in the story frame to tell about the story.

Title of the Story:	Characters:

Beginning:

Middle:

Ending:

Harcourt Brace School Publishers

FULL SAILS Practice Book

Name _____

Some describing words tell **how many.**
Some tell **what color.**

Write words from the box to complete the sentences. Then color the snowman to match your sentences.

Number Words	Color Words
1 one	red
2 two	black
3 three	blue
4 four	green

_____

- -

1. My snowman will have _____ brown
   branches.   _____

   -

2. I will give him one _____ nose.

   _____

   -

3. He will have a _____ hat.

   _____

   -

4. My snowman will have _____ things
   in all.

A. Write the Spelling Words in their shapes.

look

put

said

with

1. [   ][ ]

2. [   ][   ]

3. [   ][   ]

4. [   ][ ]

B. Write a Spelling Word to complete the rhyme.

What a good *book*!

_____

Come and have a _____.

Harcourt Brace School Publishers

Name _____

Read the weather report. Write the contraction that makes sense in each sentence.

_____

1. _____ had a week of sun.

    We've   I'll

_____

2. Now _____ going to get some snow.

    she'd   we're

_____

3. If _____ going out tonight,

    you're   we've

_____

_____ better have a hat on!

    you'd   I've

4. _____ just stay home!

    You've   I'd

Harcourt Brace School Publishers

Read each sentence. Write the word that best completes the sentence.

How to Make a Snowman

_____

- -

1. Pile up some _____.

               slow   snow

_____

- -

2. Add a _____ hat.

        small   stall

_____

- -

3. Add buttons for a _____.

           spill   smile

_____

- -

4. Put a _____ on the neck.

       skate   scarf

_____

- -

5. _____ on a carrot nose.

    Stick   Stop

Harcourt Brace School Publishers

Name _____

Read each sentence. Then read the word under it. Add the letters *ing* or *ed* to the word to complete the sentence. Don't forget to drop the <u>e</u>!

_____

- -

1. Here is Joey _____ the snow.

move

_____

- -

2. Teddy is _____ on his back.

ride

_____

- -

3. They _____ up a lot of snow.

pile

_____

- -

4. Joey is _____ .

smile

But where is Teddy?

_____

- -

5. Teddy is _____ .

hide

Name _____

Read each clue. Write the word that fits the clue and has the same vowel sound as _kite_.

1. Tick-tock, look at the clock.

_____

- -

You will see the _____.

time   hands   night

2. You can ride on me.

_____

- -

Climb on! I'm a _____.

mile   bike   skate

3. Add four and one.

_____

- -

Then you'll have me. I am _____.

six   nine   five

4. I'm here when day is over.

_____

- -

I am _____.

night   bright   now

Make your own vocabulary word game card, and cut it out. Then use paper squares to cover the words while playing "Bingo."

BINGO BINGO BINGO

BINGO

BINGO

BINGO

BINGO

BINGO

BINGO

BINGO BINGO BINGO

alone	another	miss	morning	moved
open	past	someday	wrote	

BINGO   BINGO   BINGO   BINGO   BINGO

BINGO   BINGO   BINGO   BINGO

Name _____

Think about what Jenny saw on her trip. Fill in the web. Write or draw what Jenny saw.

On her trip at sea,
Jenny saw

SCIENCE

Name _____

Some describing words tell how things **feel.**
Some tell how things **sound.**

**Write words from the box to complete
the sentences.**

hot	soft	loud
cold	hard	quiet

I Can Hear and **Feel**

_____

- -

I like it when it is _____ outside. My hands

_____

- -

can feel when something is _____. I can

_____

- -

hear a truck that is very _____. I can't hear

_____

- -

a mouse because it is very _____.

Name _____

A. Circle the Spelling Words hidden in the puzzle.

| now | of | come | one |

a	s	f	o	f
r	n	p	n	t
c	o	m	e	f
p	w	b	t	r

B. Write the Spelling Words in their shapes to complete the sentences.

1. Look at me ⬜⬜⬜.

2. I'm on top ⬜⬜ the boat.

3. I am the only ⬜⬜⬜ up here.

4. You can ⬜⬜⬜⬜.

Harcourt Brace School Publishers

Name _____

Read each sentence. Write the word that best completes the sentence.

_____
- -
1. I need my bat, ball, and _____.

             mitt   boat

_____
- -
2. But my room is a _____.

             must   mess

_____
- -
3. I will _____ more to the pile.

        ask   add

_____
- -
4. Look! Jess found my mitt with no _____!

             fuss   fast

_____
- -
5. How did I _____ seeing it?

       miss   most

Name _____

The pictures show the beginning and the middle of a story. Write sentences to tell what happens. Draw what happens at the end. Write about your ending for the story.

_____
_____
_____
_____
_____

_____
_____
_____
_____

_____
_____
_____
_____
_____
_____

Name _____

Use words from the box to complete the story.

best	last	went
ant	felt	past

_____

----

1. Grant _____ like going on a trip.

_____

----

2. So away he _____.

_____

----

3. He walked _____ a rock.

_____

----

4. At _____ he walked up a big blue shoe.

_____

----

5. "That's the _____ trip I've had!"

Name _____

Choose the word from the box that completes each riddle. Change the word so it ends in the letters *ing* or *ed.* Don't forget to drop the _e_!

| hike | smile | dance | hide |

You can't see me.
I won't let you find me.
_____
- -
I am _____.

I moved my feet along with a song.
_____
- -
I _____.

I am happy.
Look at my face.
_____
- -
I am _____.

I walked up a hill. Then I walked back down again.
_____
- -
I _____.

Read the paragraph. Write how many places Penny stopped. Then circle the words that start with *bl, sl, fl, cl,* and *pl.* Write them on the chart.

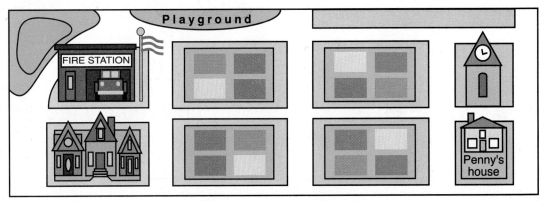

Penny left home. She stopped at the big clock. Penny went two blocks. She stopped at the flagpole. Next, Penny went to play at the playground. She slid down the slide. Then Penny went to her grandma's house. Her house is blue.

Penny stopped in ☐ places.

bl	
sl	
fl	
cl	
pl	

Name _____

**Read each question. Then write a word from
the box to answer each one.**

boat	home	coat	rose	joke

_____
- -

1. Where do you live? _____

_____
- -

2. What can you grow? _____

_____
- -

3. What can you ride in? _____

_____
- -

4. What can you put on? _____

_____
- -

5. What might make you smile? _____

Harcourt Brace School Publishers

SKILLS AND STRATEGIES INDEX

How to make a Learning Log 1–2

DECODING
Phonic analysis
  Consonant correspondences
    Clusters, initial
      with *l* 8, 26, 76
      with *s* 64
    Clusters, final
      -ld, -mp, -nd 53
      with *t* 16, 55, 74
    Digraph
      /sh/*sh*, /hw/*wh* 34, 46, 57
    Final
      /d/*dd*, /t/*tt*, /s/*ss* 72
    Medial
      /d/*d*, /l/*l*, /n/*n*, /s/*s* 54
  Vowel correspondences
    /ē/*e, ea, ee* 44
    /e/*e*, /a/*a* 10
    /ī/*i, i-e, igh* 35, 56, 66
    /ō/*o, oa, o-e* 17, 27, 77
Structural analysis
  Contractions
    've, 're, 'd 63
  Inflections
    -ed, -ing 24, 65, 75
  Possessive
    's 25

VOCABULARY
Key Words 3-4, 11-12, 19-20, 29-30, 39-40, 48-49, 58-59, 67-68

COMPREHENSION
Main idea and details 45
Making predictions 9, 28, 37
Summarize and retell 5, 13, 21, 31, 41, 50, 60, 69
Summarizing and retelling 36

LITERARY APPRECIATION
Story elements 73

STUDY SKILLS
Alphabetical order 18, 38, 47

GRAMMAR
Describing words 32, 42
  colors and numbers 61
  feel and sound 70
  size, shape, taste, smell 51
Special naming words
  He, she, and *it* 22
  I and *me* 14
  months and holidays 6

SPELLING
Words with
  short *a* 43
  short *e* 7
  short *i* 23
  short *o* 52
  short *u* 15
  wh 33
Words to remember 62
Words to remember with *o* 71